Hurricanes

By Jim Gigliotti

The Child's World®
www.childsworld.com

Published in the United States of America by The Child's World®
P.O. Box 326 • Chanhassen, MN 55317-0326
800-599-READ • www.childsworld.com

Thanks to Kate Wentzel, chief meteorologist for KEYT-TV in
Santa Barbara, Calif., for offering her expertise during the
creation of this book.

ACKNOWLEDGMENTS

The Child's World®: Mary Berendes, Publishing Director

Produced by Shoreline Publishing Group LLC
President / Editorial Director: James Buckley, Jr.
Designer: Tom Carling, carlingdesign.com
Cover Art: Slimfilms
Copy Editor: Beth Adelman

Photo Credits
Cover—Main, inset center right: Corbis; inset upper right:
    Photos.com; other insets: AP/Wide World
Interior—AP/Wide World: 16, 21, 22, 27; Corbis: 8, 19, 25, 29;
Dreamstime.com: 7; Getty Images: 5, 13, 18; iStock: 15, 26;
Photos.com: 10

LIBRARY OF CONGRESS CATALOGING-IN-PUBLICATION DATA

Gigliotti, Jim.
  Hurricanes / by Jim Gigliotti.
    p. cm. — (Boys rock!)
  Includes bibliographical references and index.
  ISBN 1-59296-731-0 (library bound : alk. paper)
  1. Hurricanes—Juvenile literature. I. Title. II. Series.
  QC944.2.G54 2006
  551.55'2—dc22
                        2006004604

CONTENTS

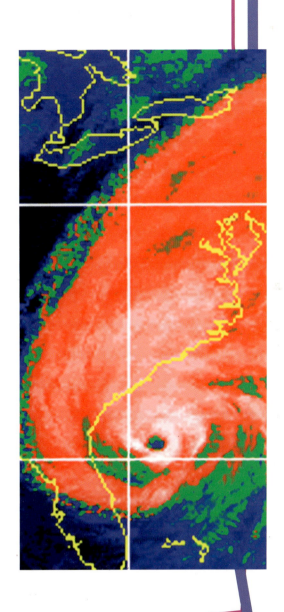

THE BIGGEST Storms

The wind howled at 125 miles (201 km) per hour. The rain poured down—as much as 15 inches (38 cm) in some areas. Huge areas were flooded. It was "the storm we always feared," as one New Orleans newspaper wrote. The storm was Hurricane Katrina. It was the most **destructive** hurricane ever to hit the United States. Hurricanes are terrible storms that can cause

widespread damage. Katrina hit the coast of Louisiana on Monday, August 29, 2005. Thousands were left homeless. Many people were killed. Katrina was an example of hurricanes at their worst. Let's learn more about these amazing storms.

On a normal day, this New Orleans street would be full of cars and people. This photo shows it during Hurricane Katrina.

The first major hurricane of each year is given a male or female name that starts with the letter A. After that, the list of names for the year goes through the alphabet. (Uncommon letters such as Q and X are skipped.)

Not all hurricanes are as destructive as Katrina. Still, hurricanes are among the most dangerous storms in the world.

Hurricanes produce extremely strong winds that can reach speeds of more than 155 miles (249 km) per hour. Short bursts of high winds, called *gusts*, can also do damage. It's not just the winds that make hurricanes so terrifying, though. Hurricanes can dump many, many inches of rain on an area in a short time. They can also push ocean water inland, which is called a *storm surge*. That water can pour into coastal communities. Along with waves created by the wind, the surge can flood homes and streets.

Even the strongest trees were no match for the high winds of Hurricane Rita in 2005.

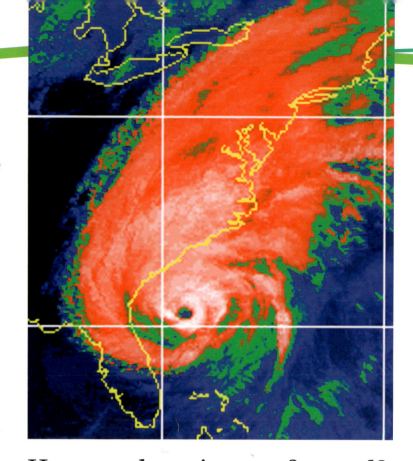

This picture, taken from high above the earth, shows a hurricane moving along the eastern coast of the United States. The red-and-white swirl is the hurricane, and the yellow line is the coastline of the eastern United States.

How are hurricanes formed? The key is **air pressure**. That's the force that holds large masses of air together. When air pressure is very low, the air in that area can cause high winds to blow around it. These high winds are created when high-pressure areas meet up with the low-pressure areas. The winds blow around these low-pressure areas. As those winds blow faster and faster, a serious storm develops.

Most hurricanes begin as **tropical storms**. Low-pressure areas form these storms in warm, moist areas of the world. They are called tropical storms once their winds reach 39 miles (63 km) per hour. If their winds speed up to 74 miles (119 km) per hour, the storms become a hurricane.

These storms have different names in different parts of the world. In the Atlantic and eastern Pacific, they are hurricanes. In the western Pacific, they are called typhoons. In the Indian Ocean, they are known as cyclones.

An average hurricane has a **radius** (the distance from its center to its edge) of about 300 miles (483 km). The largest hurricane to hit the United States was in 1979 and had a radius of 675 miles (1,086 km)!

This photo, taken from space, shows the clouds of a huge hurricane circling around its center.

Hurricanes move at different speeds. They can move slowly enough to let people prepare for them. They can also go as fast as 60 miles (97 km) per hour.

The word *hurricane* comes from the name of a native Caribbean storm god, Huracan.

Hurricanes need warm water to continue their journey. Once they reach land, they lose most of their strength. Katrina first touched land in Florida as a much weaker hurricane. As it passed over the Gulf of Mexico, it picked up power from the water and turned into a major hurricane.

The middle of a hurricane is called its *eye*. If you imagine a hurricane as a giant doughnut, the eye is the hole in the doughnut. Remember the low-pressure area? The eye is that area, and high winds spin around it.

Now imagine that you are sitting inside that doughnut hole. Winds are swirling all around you. Inside the eye, though, it's just a bit breezy and you might even be able to see some blue sky, or maybe stars if it's night. It's almost peaceful.

Don't be fooled, though. The eye of the hurricane is just a brief pause. The edges of that hole will soon pass over you. In a hurricane, the edge of the eye is called the *eye wall*—and that's where you'll find the strongest winds and the heaviest rain.

Hurricanes often cause flooding. This car near New Orleans was left floating after Katrina hit.

2

TYPES OF Hurricanes

Hurricanes are given numbers from 1 to 5, depending on how strong they are. **Category** 5 hurricanes have much stronger winds than Category 1 hurricanes. But Category 1 hurricanes are still pretty strong! They have winds that blow from 74 to 95 miles (119 to 153 km) per hour—hard enough to blow leaves off trees. Category 2 hurricanes have winds from 96 to 110 miles (154 to

177 km) per hour. These winds can knock over large signs and rip branches off trees. When their winds reach 111 to 130 miles (179 to 209 km) per hour, hurricanes move into Category 3 and are considered "major." They can damage buildings and blow down large trees.

Hurricane Rita was a Category 5 storm. Its strong winds badly damaged these palm trees.

Hurricane Katrina sent ocean water rolling over this Mississippi coastal town, destroying much of it.

Category 4 hurricanes have winds that blow even faster—131 to 155 miles (211 to 249 km) per hour. They can cause lots of damage, including tearing roofs off smaller buildings and flooding homes and buildings near the seashore.

Category 5 hurricanes are the most destructive, with winds of over 155 miles (249 km) per hour. They blow the roofs off buildings. After a Category 5 hurricane, many buildings must be torn down because they are too damaged. Fortunately, Category 5 hurricanes are rare. Only six have reached that level near the United States since 1935. Four of them—Emily, Katrina, Rita, and Wilma— all hit the Gulf Coast in 2005, though they had "calmed" to Category 3 by the time they hit.

Still, those four hurricanes —and others—were big news in 2005. The Atlantic Ocean usually has about six hurricanes a year, two of them "major" (Category 3 or higher). In 2005, however, there were 15 hurricanes. Seven of them were major. It was the most active hurricane season in the Atlantic Ocean since people started keeping records.

By any measure, Hurricane Katrina was probably the worst of all of those. At least 1,600 people died, and

property damage amounted to $75 billion.

Before Katrina, the costliest hurricane to hit the United States was Andrew. Its high winds swept across Florida in 1992, causing $26.5 billion in damage.

In 1992, the Category 5 Hurricane Andrew destroyed houses like these in Florida.

The deadliest hurricane in the United States hit Galveston, Texas, in 1900. It was a Category 4 storm that killed about 8,000 people.

The city is located on a low, sand island on the southern coast of Texas. The storm surge and high winds roared over the island and caused great destruction.

The high loss of life in the Galveston **disaster** came in part because people didn't fully understand what sort of storm was coming. Though they are not perfect, today's **forecasters** are much better at knowing exactly where and when a hurricane will hit. People can prepare for the coming storms.

3

BE
Prepared

Who's most likely to be affected by
hurricanes? People who live along the
Atlantic Ocean and the Gulf of Mexico.

'Tis the Season

Hurricane season in the Atlantic Ocean runs from June 1 to November 30 each year. That's when the water temperatures are at their warmest.

Hurricanes can hit those areas hard, while the storms still have lots of power. After they hit land, hurricanes lose power. Even so, they can still produce heavy rain and tornadoes. For people who live in many areas, preparing for hurricanes is simply a fact of life. To help people get ready, scientists have become better at **predicting** hurricanes.

OPPOSITE PAGE:
Before Hurricane Lily hit Louisiana in 2002, this shop owner put up wood to protect his windows.

Predicting means saying what is going to happen in the future.

In fact, there is a system for warning people about hurricanes. A *hurricane watch* tells people that a hurricane might hit sometime in their area in the next 36 hours. A *hurricane warning* tells people that a hurricane is going to hit within 24 hours. In some cases, people might be told to leave the area, or **evacuate**. This simple system has saved many lives—especially as scientists have gotten better at figuring out what hurricanes will do. Even when people know hurricanes are coming, getting out of the way can be hard. Hurricane Katrina was predicted, but the evacuation did not go well and created problems.

This worker at the National Hurricane Center used computers and many other tools to track Katrina in 2005.

Signs like these can help people find the fastest and safest route away from the path of a hurricane.

If you live in an area where hurricanes occur, the best thing you can do is be prepared. Listen for hurricane watches and warnings, and evacuate immediately when you and your family are told to do so.

Having a family disaster kit is a good idea, too. Hurricanes often shut down power and water supplies. Your disaster kit might contain such things as canned food (don't forget a can opener!), water, flashlights, and a radio. Fuel, candles, matches, and batteries help provide light. Include a first-aid kit, too. The things in your disaster kit can help you and your family until your house has power and water again.

Along with food, water, and flashlights, keep a battery-powered radio in your disaster kit.

Being in a hurricane can be a scary thing. But many people are helping to keep others safe from these storms. One kind of scientist actually flies in an airplane into the middle of a hurricane. These "Hurricane Hunters" are part of the Air Force Reserves. They use special equipment on their planes to study hurricanes.

The pilots say the scariest part is flying into the eye wall, where the winds are strongest. That makes for a bumpy flight!

Hurricane Hunters—and others—will keep studying hurricanes. They want to understand more about these powerful storms—and how to keep people safe!

Special propeller planes take Hurricane Hunters right into the clouds of a hurricane.

GLOSSARY

air pressure the force that holds large masses of air together

category a group of things that are very similar

destructive causing a lot of damage and destroying many things

disaster a disaster is when something terrible happens

evacuate leave an area in a hurry, usually to escape a dangerous situation

forecasters scientists who study the weather and its patterns

predicting thinking about what will happen in the future based on information from the present

radius the distance from the center of a circle (or a hurricane) to its edge

tropical storms storms formed by moist, warm air that have wind speeds of 39 to 73 miles (63 to 117 km) per hour

FIND OUT MORE

BOOKS

Eyewitness Hurricane & Tornado
    by Jack Challoner
    (DK Publishing, New York) 2000
    This book includes lots of photos, drawings, and information
    on hurricanes.

Hurricanes
    by Seymour Simon
    (HarperCollins, New York) 2003
    A popular science writer explains how hurricanes develop and
    how they affect people.

The Magic School Bus Inside a Hurricane
    by Joanna Cole
    (Scholastic, Inc., New York) 1995
    Take a magical trip inside a hurricane to see how these storms
    develop.

WEB SITES

Visit our home page for lots of links about hurricanes:
    www.childsworld.com/links

Note to Parents, Teachers, and Librarians: We routinely check our Web links to make sure they're safe, active sites—so encourage your readers to check them out!

INDEX

Jim Gigliotti is a writer who lives in southern California with his wife and two children. He has written more than a dozen books for youngsters and adults on topics such as football, baseball, auto racing, and firefighters.